ANGELS ON HORSEBACK

Angels on Horseback

~ and else~where

by thelwell

METHUEN & CO LTD

FIRST PUBLISHED SEPTEMBER 19TH 1957
REPRINTED TWICE 1958
REPRINTED FIVE TIMES
REPRINTED 1969
BY METHUEN & CO LTD
11 NEW FETTER LANE, EC4
PRINTED IN GREAT BRITAIN
BY LATIMER TREND & CO LTD
WHITSTABLE

SBN 416 59970 2

1.9

For
DAVID & PENNY

Most of the pictures originally appeared in *Punch* and are published here by kind permission of the proprietors.

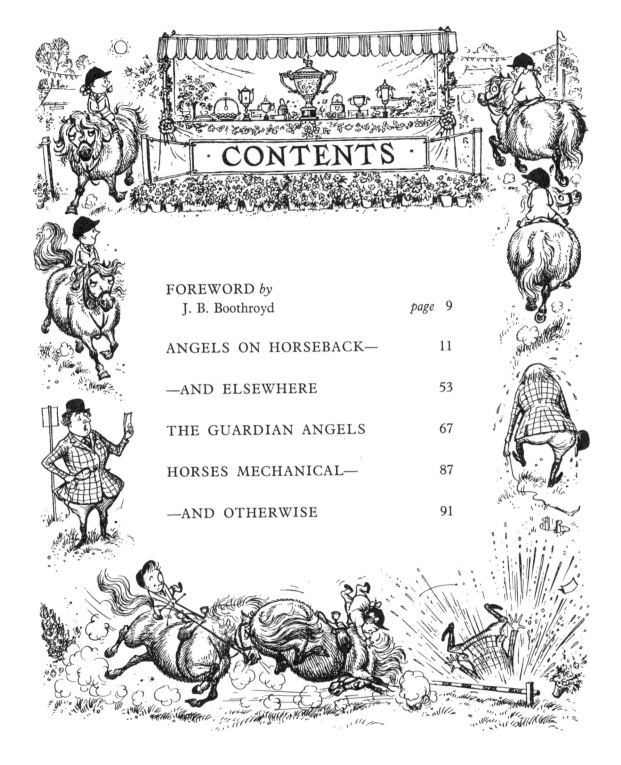

· CONTENTS ·

" Now the fall is important."

FOREWORD

THERE was a song, 'Crazy Over Horses'. They weren't Thelwell's kind, but the kind that exist on shaved green turf for the few, the back page of the evening papers for the many—and for him nowhere. He doesn't recognize them. His horses never brought a grandstand to its feet, clashing binoculars. Brains are not blown out over them. Yet they are the horses that people who know horses know.

I do not know horses. But I have come nearer to it through these drawings than in any other way. For me they have humanized both horses and horsepeople—and if you think there is no such thing as a human horse, eavesdrop at the nearest Hunt Ball. As a lifelong non-equestrian I have suffered many a pang of inferiority, because there is something terribly crushing about anyone on a horse. Even a home-going labourer clomping past me in a country lane, side-saddle and bareback (if that can be), tempts me to touch my forelock, and astounds me by touching his first.

No doubt it's something to do with the height. The rider can't help looking down on the rest of the world, and it is easy to imagine that he is looking down his own nose as well as the horse's. However, I know at last that is not so. Thelwell has convinced me, and I can never be too grateful, that the horse person is, if possible, even less sure of himself than I am. Even those russet-coloured lumps on horses' backs that prove, as they jog into focus, to be small children in tiny velvet caps and impeccable little Jodhpurs which they must be literally growing out of every second, hold no terrors for me now. They are revealed as palpitating bundles of exposed nerve-ends, liable to be shot through a blackthorn hedge any minute like a stone from a catapult. This comforts me. In future, instead of avoiding the eye of middle-aged ladies with bowler hats and Roman noses who gallop at me round the blind corners of Sussex byways, I shall watch them keenly out of sight. Thelwell may have a disaster arranged for them.

Punch has had equestrian artists before. In mid-Victorian times it was difficult to open a copy without being trampled. But the creations between these present covers achieve something entirely new: they combine portraiture with caricature, a thing which most artists would hesitate to try with human beings, let alone the more temperamentally elusive and psychologically inscrutable horse. This means that while no horse could possibly look exactly like a Thelwell horse, all Thelwell horses manage to look exactly like horses. If anyone can explain this, or express it more lucidly, they should write to the publishers, please, not me

To end with a reminder that Thelwell is not only an artist but a humorist is not to suggest that anyone could overlook it, but to make it clear that I haven't. It is hard for one practising humorist to praise another . . . but how is it that all these centuries have gone by without anyone thinking of the joke on page 51? Or 60? Or, for that matter ——?

But, anyway, they're all yours now.

J. B. Boothroyd

ANGELS ON HORSEBACK

Booted and Spurned
A GUIDE TO BRITISH PONY BREEDS

1. *DARTMOOR AND EXMOOR*
Though inclined to be wild—these ponies make lovable mounts if taken from the moors early enough.

2. *CONNEMARA.* Mostly grey nowadays—are among the oldest inhabitants of the British Isles.

3. *NEW FOREST.* Due to the abundance of traffic in the area—
this rather narrow breed is said to be immune to the terror of
modern roads.

4. *WELSH
MOUNTAIN*
Perhaps the most
beautiful of our native
ponies but it is
debatable whether the
' dished' face line is due
to Arab influence.

5. *FELL AND DALE*. Originally used to carry lead—are ideal for the larger family.

6. *HIGHLAND*. The largest and strongest and quite unrivalled in surefootedness.

7. *SHETLAND*.   The smallest and hardiest breed of all and
perfect for introducing children to the problems of horsemanship.

17

" 'ow do *they* feel then? "

" I see you've kicked the toes out of them already."

Small in the Saddle
A FEW POINTERS WHEN BUYING A PONY

1. A child regards his first pony as a new plaything.

2. They must suit each other in temperament

3. Experience is needed when buying from public auctions

4. It is not always easy to recognise a good pony " in the rough".

5. The mount should not be
too wide for the child's
short legs.

6. Daily exercise is most
important

7. And careful grooming
essential to the pony's happiness

Anyway, it's a wonderful way for a child to learn how to enjoy
Man's mastery over nature.

Look before you Leap
A CHILD'S GUIDE TO SHOW-JUMPING

The opportunity to examine the fences before the start of the competition should never be missed.

The signal to start is given by a bell, flag or whistle.

Look before you Leap
A CHILD'S GUIDE TO SHOW-JUMPING

A horse or pony is said to have " REFUSED " if he stops in front
of a fence . . .

. . . and to have " FALLEN " if the shoulders and quarters have
touched the ground.

Look before you Leap
A CHILD'S GUIDE TO SHOW-JUMPING

A competitor is eliminated for showing any fence to a horse after a refusal.

Or for unauthorised assistance whether solicited or not.

Look before you Leap
A CHILD'S GUIDE TO SHOW-JUMPING

Endless patience is required to reach perfection.

But for those who ultimately achieve a clear round—the rewards are many.

Horse Show
AT THE WHITE CITY

Miss Pam Smith on the famous " Tusker " enters the arena.

Willowbrook Show

ON THE GREEN

Shirley Wilkinson and " Tearaway " enter the ring.

Horse Show
AT THE WHITE CITY

Mr. Robinson's " Firebird " taking the water.

Willowbrook Show
ON THE GREEN

Tom Jenkins' " Thistledown " taking the water.

Horse Show
AT THE WHITE CITY

Col. Boyce-Partington on "Prince Consort" at the wall.

Willowbrook Show
ON THE GREEN

Four-year-old Penelope Bright riding " Nimble "
tackles an obstacle.

Horse Show
AT THE WHITE CITY

The Marquis of Basingstoke presented the trophies.

Willowbrook Show
ON THE GREEN

" Well jumped Mary ", laughed Mrs. Hornby-James
who presented the prizes.

" I'm sorry I ever mentioned he'd got a stone in his hoof."

"HEEL!"

~And Elsewhere

" What have I told you about drawing on the walls? "

" You rang? "

". . . and hurry . . ."

The Guardian Angels

68

" Charles ! Did you ask anyone to meet you here this morning? "

" Increasing mechanisation of the countryside is enabling more
and more people to afford the luxury of owning . . . .

. . . a horse."

" Just *look* at it! ' Lacks initiative . . .
Easily dominated . . .' "

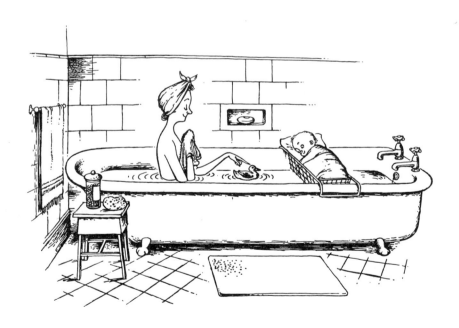

" Same again George."

Horses Mechanical

" Pretty-pretty."

" Give Fred a shout as you go by—he's doing the traffic census."